Beautiful Games

Heiner Thofern

Beautiful Games

Roman Entrances

Steidl

Roman entrances from the time of the "miracolo economico italiano" – from beautiful game to game over?

Heiner Thofern

"Roma", a city name that easily evokes associations in almost everyone: the Colosseum, Pantheon, St. Peter's Basilica, Piazza Navona, Trevi Fountain and Dolce Vita on Via Veneto – all places in the heart of the Italian capital. And so, it is no coincidence that the attention of travelers to Rome is concentrated on the historic city centre enclosed by the Aurelian city walls. The most famous ruins of antiquity and the magnificent buildings of the Renaissance and Baroque are gathered here. The abundance and extraordinary quality of these sights undoubtedly justify this focus of interest.

Nevertheless, anyone who wants to get to know the Rome of today has to look far beyond the city centre. The historic downtown, dominated by tourism, now makes up only a tiny fraction of the city's urban area with 1.5 percent, and just around 125,000 of Rome's 2.8 million inhabitants still live there.

The majority of everyday life in Rome unfolds beyond the ancient city walls. In the post-war period, especially during the years of the Italian economic miracle between 1951 and 1971, Rome's population grew by 1.1 to 2.7 million. This was associated with a construction boom[1] that caused the built-up urban area to grow like a spreading oil stain. One of the main features of this development was a flourishing building speculation. Accordingly, ugliness and triviality dominate many of the neighbourhoods which developed at that time.

On the other hand, one will also find outstanding buildings of great elegance and memorablility there.[2] The attentive observer will soon notice a genuinely Roman building type: the *palazzina*. This is a free-standing building with a maximum of four to five storeys, the facades of which are all thoroughly designed. Especially the upscale residential areas from the 1950s to 1970s in the Roman north (Vigna Clara, Cassia, Pinciano, Parioli, Salario-Trieste, Nomentano and Talenti) and west (EUR, Monteverde, Balduina and Monte Mario) are characterised by this building type.

The often lavish and imaginatively designed entrance areas of these buildings deserve special attention. During the day most entrances are hidden from view from the outside because their glass doors reflect the surrounding streetscape.

But after dark, with the interior lighting switched on, they reveal themselves to passers-by in all their richness. In many instances, the transition from the public to the increasingly private realm is masterly staged. Those arriving are prepared for the building. Large sculptures, wall-filling reliefs or mosaics lead to the main entrance. Catchy geometrically shaped metal gates mark the threshold to the inside of the building. The highlights are the entrance areas themselves: carefully composed stone floors, elaborate wall claddings, mosaics, sculptures, ceramic lighting fixtures and fountains are just as much a part of the repertoire as extravagant banisters, elegant letterboxes and Janus-headed (half inside, half outside) porters' lodges. Curved staircases, slight differences in level, and elevator shafts housed in free-standing cylinders create sophisticated spatial sequences resulting in what can felicitously be called a truly beautiful game.

These entrances are genuine visiting cards for the building. They communicate the status of their residents. The building contractors, intent on maximising profits, gave the architects a wide range of design options in order to give the *palazzine* that certain something (*dare un tono*), which corresponded to the striving for prestige of potential buyers. Outstanding architectural firms even consulted well-known artists when designing the entrance areas.[3]

The Roman entrances from the years of the Italian economic miracle form an architectural legacy that hardly finds any equivalent in contemporary building design. Today, entrance areas are for the most part soberly reduced to the bare essentials. Spacious atriums are considered a waste of space; elaborate planning of details remains the great exception. This tendency is also reflected in the apartment floor plans themselves: where one was once received in spacious hallways, there is now often no transition zone at all. Rather, one enters the living space directly through the apartment entrance door (*salone all'americana*). This not only applies to new buildings, but is also frequently seen in apartment renovations. In order to increase the living space, the hall is often added to the main living room. The resulting artistic impoverishment is just one more reason to call to mind the quality of this architectural heritage, not least in the hope that this might help prevent the aforementioned beautiful game to ultimately be a "game over".

1 The entrance wall mosaic on pp. 92-93 celebrates this construction boom, picturing the huge ground works carried out by a typical Rome manufactured Fiorentini excavator of that time, and showing the predominant reinforced concrete skeleton construction method.

2 It is no coincidence that many of these buildings were used as film sets soon after their completion. Examples are the iconic Il Girasole designed by Luigi Moretti in the episode "Gli italiani si voltano/Italians Stare" directed by Alberto Lattauda in the anthology film *Amore in città/ Love in the City* (1953), the Villino on Via Appiano by Ugo Luccichenti in Dino Risi's *Il sorpasso/ The Easy Life* (1962), the elegant apartment building by Francesco Berarducci on Via dei Colli della Farnesina in *Indagine su un cittadino al di sopra di ogni sospetto/Investigation of a Citizen Above Suspicion* (1970), the Casa Papanice by Paolo Portoghesi on Via Giuseppe Marchi in Ettore Scola's *Dramma della gelosia/The Pizza Triangle* (1970) and in Sergio Martino's *Lo strano vizio della signora Wardh/The Strange Vice of Mrs. Wardh* (1971), and the condominium building known as *La Nave* (ship) on Via Guglielmo Mengarini by Pier Giorgio Stefani in Elio Petri's *La proprietà non è più and furto/Property Is No Longer a Theft* (1973).

3 Vincenzo Monaco and Amedeo Luccichenti, for example, worked with Pietro Consagra (Via Archimede, Via Valentino, Via del Circo Massimo, Viale Parioli, Via San Crescenziano) and Pietro Cascella (Via Ximenes), Julio Lafuente with Andrea and Pietro Cascella and Annamaria Cesarini Sforza (Viale di Trastevere), Luigi Moretti with Claire Falkenstein (Via Giovanni Battista Morgagni), Ildo Avetta with Leonardo Leoncillo (Viale Regina Margherita), Eugenio Galdieri with Piero Dorazio and Achille Perilli (Via Valpolicella), Mario Marchi with Enzo Assenza (Via Achille Papa) or Giorgio Calza Bini with Luigi Scirocchi (Viale Beethoven). Not to forget the architect and artist couple Massimo Parboni Arquati and Serena Boselli.

10

INTE
35
VOI AVETE SCELTO
LA VOSTRA NUOVA CASA.
INSIEME POSSIAMO COMPLETARLA.
1,15%
LAFURIA!

121

38
Avv ETTORE VERGINELLI
STUDIO LEGALE

"Being Latin and 'catholic' as opposed to austere and 'protestant', and having been nourished on the richness of the Renaissance and weaned on the extravagance of the Baroque, this new Italian architecture ... has a richness and sensuousness unknown to our nordic climates."

George Everard Kidder Smith, 1956

21

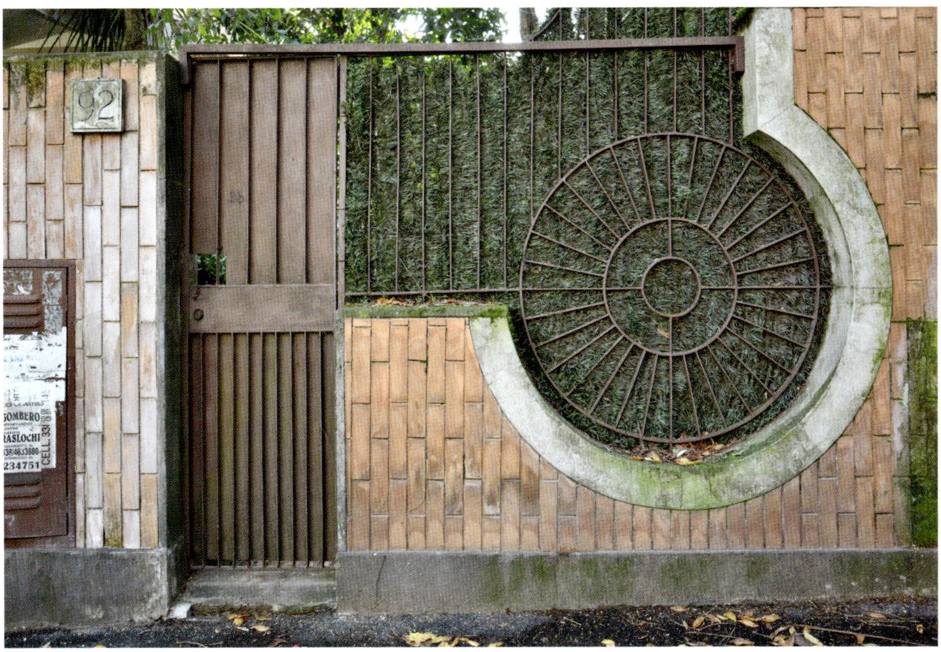
92

27

DENTISTI ASSOCIATI
CONFALONE
IMPLANTOLOGIA
ORTODONZIA - PROTESI
DIGITALE
Tel. 06 6382814
Via dei SAVORELLI 54 - Via MARCELLO II N.22
Scala D Int. 5
(Piazza PIO XI) parcheggio riservato
www.dentistiassociaticonfalone.it
Dr.ssa Roberta Ristagno
Psicologa Psicoterapeuta
Prof. a.c. Facoltà Medicina e Chirurgia
Univ. La Sapienza Roma
Tel. 328.8980146

D.ssa Valerija Evetovic
LOGOPEDISTA
scala D interno 5
STUDIO DENTISTICO CONFALONE
tel. 06.6382814 cell. 3939400689
VENDESI
TRASLOCHI
SGOMBERI
339 2501353
SERRANDE
320 8182793

OZTERIA
4
3
2

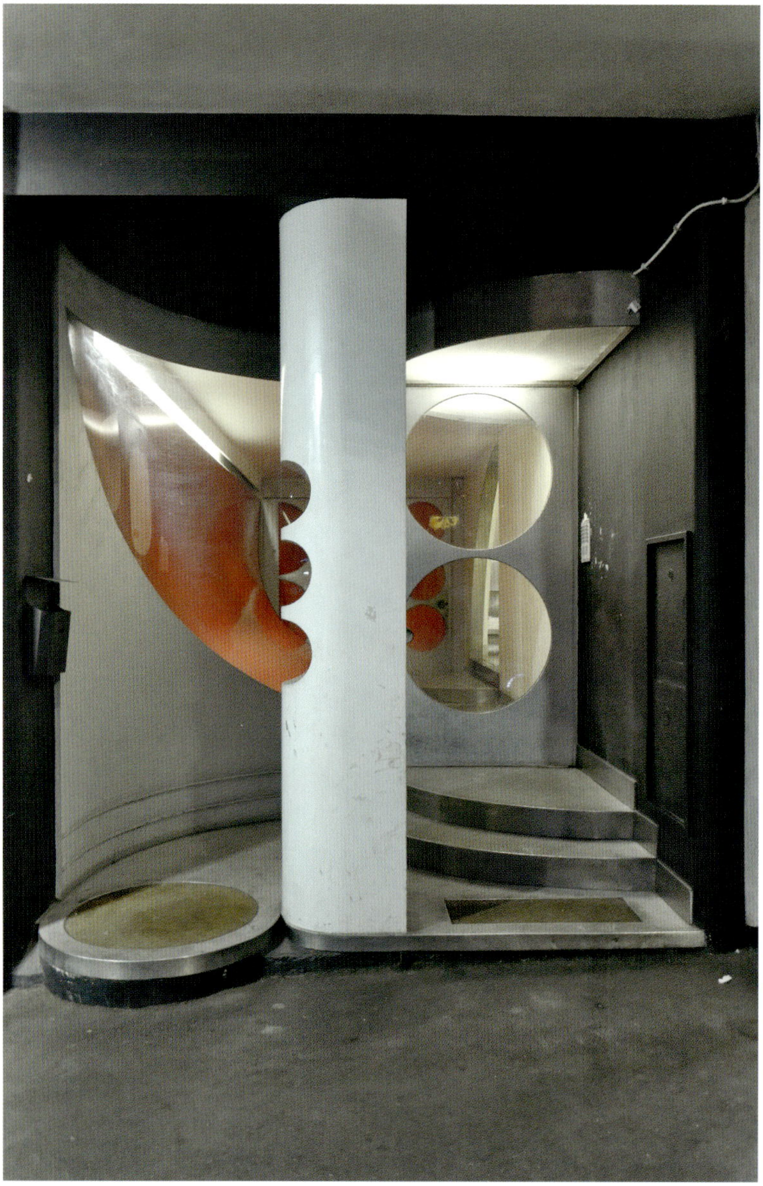

26

"In the post-war period in Rome ... architects ... participated in the ongoing regeneration of all sectors of Italian economic and cultural life in the season in which beauty became a reason for commitment."

Raffaele Giannantonio, 2014

"architecture represents ... the aesthetic side of building ... Beauty in a profound sense is an essential factor in human life."

Lucio Passarelli, 2010

“from the postwar period up to the 1960s there was talk ... of an architectural culture, of a proper Roman architecture ... Rome appeared, and really was, a laboratory of ideas and proposals in full and intense ferment open on a 360-degree horizon.”

Stefano Ray, 1990

7
8
6
14
15
10
12

"During the years of the construction boom everything was possible, everything found a correspondence, as if a dream came true"

Piergiorgio Stefani, 2020

Roman entrance halls: a place for experimental dialogue between art and architecture

Elisabetta Cristallini

Following the Second World War, the city of Rome took on a new physiognomy. Pier Paolo Pasolini with his books and films (from *The Ragazzi* to *The Hawks and the Sparrows*) became the voice of the capital's great urban transformation. In the years before well-being, speculative construction and an alienating consumer society, the city's beauty was still firmly intact and positively enchanting, thanks to that incomparable palimpsest of monuments, ruins, countryside, stately and less stately buildings, working-class neighbourhoods and the first tendrils of urban sprawl. City-dwelling country folk, residents without homes in the bombed city and war veterans became the stars of a new epos in fiction and cinema. Rome itself became the "cinema city", starting out with the quintessential anti-Hollywood film *Rome, Open City* by young director Roberto Rossellini, released in 1945, with that unforgettable scene where Anna Magnani is killed by the Nazis. Made with a very low budget and improvised scenes, the film made "an enormous and moving impression" as Federico Fellini would later recall.[1] Rome was immediately flooded with directors and actors, as well as artists and writers from all over the world. Especially Americans who adored Rome and were adored by the city in return, as we know from memorable films such as *Roman Holiday*, where Audrey Hepburn and Gregory Peck happily roam the city on a Vespa, or *An American in Rome*, which gave us Alberto Sordi's ironic interpretation of Americanisation.

Rome was livelier back then, it had greater aspirations and it stimulated more intellectual curiosity than Paris, which at the time still held the international avant-garde of art before passing the baton to New York at the height of the 1960s. Alberto Arbasino recalls: "Rome at the time was the most cosmopolitan city in Europe, in fact it was the intercontinental airport of the West, with a huge flow of visitors who still preferred Italy and the Renaissance for tourism that had yet to become mass, and a large number of foreigners who, in the old uninterrupted tradition of the English, French and Americans, permanently resided here in Tuscan villas and Roman palazzos, in Umbrian convents and the stretch of coast between Amalfi and Sorrento. There was the constant traffic of actors and directors around Cinecittà; long stays by illustrious writers and painters between Venice and Capri and Trastevere; and the very first interest in emerging Italian fashion, with soon-to-be 'legendary' names such as Simonetta Visconti and Irene Galitzine".[2]

Rome assumed, in short, a symbolic role in the epochal transformation of Italy and even Europe, as the first European capital to be liberated from Nazi fascism when American troops arrived on 4 June 1944 with General Clark at the fore. Other Italian cities, Milan included, would have to wait another year until 25 April 1945. In the name of anti-fascism, so began the post-war season in Rome where the search for the Italian identity saw extensive reflection on the role of art integrated into architecture, which contributed to the overall plan for national civic and material reconstruction. Various interventions and actions from well-known personalities also played a decisive role. Among these were Lionello Venturi (who had returned to Italy from exile in America to take the art history chair at the University of Rome), Giulio Carlo Argan (also a professor at the University of Rome), and Palma Bucarelli (director of the Galleria Nazionale d'Arte Moderna). All three were supporters of abstract (as opposed to figurative) language in art, the only language that was able to engage with architecture, breaking free from the recent past when, under fascism in the 1930s, art was used in new architecture with rhetorical and ideological purposes. Where the language of modern art was abstract, architecture embraced a reductionist, "poor" line, albeit with a different approach. Once again, a sharp break with so much past rhetoric, the idea was to start from the hypothesis of a critical revision of rationalism in order to "find a *more realistic* and more *human* dimension in the planning of new residential accommodation".[3]

Town planning, new construction, and the ethical and material reconstruction of the newly democratic country: these were the great heroes of post-war Italy. This is the context in which the dialogue between art and architecture insinuated itself, regulated as part of public construction by the 2% law, which allocated this small amount to art in all new construction.[4] The issue refers to the more complex matter of the *synthèse des arts*, as theorised by Le Corbusier, an architect (and artist) who had been involved with this since the 1920s. He was the reference point for anybody interested in the question of integrating modern art into new architecture. And in the first decade of Italy's republican history, a lively theoretical debate on the resumption of an anti-rhetorical synthesis of the arts would unfold at conferences and in magazines. Artists and architects of varying degrees of fame were involved and architectural language was influenced by the formal suggestions of widespread, modern, neo-cubist and abstract art, meaning that profiles were refined and balconies triangulated. Later, in the 1960s, with the crisis of the Modern Movement, those lines would be freed, the priority of form over function was recognised and inspiration was taken from history.[5] Nevertheless, the two languages (art and architecture) continued to coexist and intersect before firmly entrenching themselves as autonomous disciplines in the last decades of the twentieth century.

In Rome, collaborations between architects and artists, very common from the 1950s, were often the result of those involved attending the same schools and academies or frequenting the same cultural milieu and renowned "art spots" where writers, journalists, directors, actors and intellectuals to varying degrees would gather. From Via Margutta, home to many artists and their ateliers, to the bars and cafes of the historic centre (Rosati in Piazza del Popolo, Greco on Via Condotti, Notegen on Via del Babuino) and favourite lunch haunts: Osteria Cesaretto on Via della Croce and Trattoria Menghi on Via Flaminia, where the owners would offer credit in exchange for a picture from the painters or consultation from the architects. While Via Veneto, all the way to the Trevi Fountain, was the reign of the *Dolce Vita* (immortalised by Federico Fellini's film of the same name) with its cafes and nightclubs, which functioned as meeting places for intellectuals, the stars of international cinema and Italian and international magnates. Hence a shared sentiment and general sensitivity towards shapes, signs, light, colours, materials and atmosphere.

The first public occasions on which the dialogue between art and architecture really emerged followed two tenders: the first for the Monument to the Martyrs of Fosse Ardeatine, with its austere and eloquent shrine and dramatic and intense gates by Mirko Basaldella; the second for the finishing touches to Termini Station, with a bold large atrium (offset so as not to disturb the ancient Servian walls from the sixth century BC), decorated with an external frieze by Amerigo Tot.

However, an interesting new area for experimentation with this dialogue in the capital, testimony to widespread inventive creativity, was a new construction type: the *palazzina*. An alternative to both the upper-class villa and the working-class residence, the *palazzina* was aimed at the middle and upper-middle classes who sought both identity and status symbols. It was a typically Roman phenomenon dating back to the 1920s. Although the building must respect specific dimensions regulated by law, each architect and client could then build the *palazzina* as they liked, with no formal constraints and the use of carefully designed details and materials. This meant that no two were alike. These *palazzine* were initially found around the historic centre but after the Second World War they spread further afield to conquer new neighbourhoods where constraints and regulations were ignored. Many saw the involvement of some of Rome's best architects and some are of incredible quality.[6] Refined shapes were matched with carefully selected colours and materials for walls, false ceilings, floors and occasionally even an art element.

A generation of architects working in the city, including Ernesto Lapadula, Vincenzo Monaco, Amedeo and Ugo Luccichenti, Eugenio Galdieri, Julio Lafuente, Eugenio Montuori, Mario Ridolfi and Angelo Di Castro (as well as other lesser-known architects and engineers), asked for artistic contributions for their new *palazzine* as well as for the modernisation of cafes, restaurants, shops, cinemas and theatres – work now mostly lost due to careless subsequent renovation.[7] Some of Italy's greatest artists responded to this call and experimented with the modern language of art in the spaces of everyday life: from Gino Severini[8] to younger names such as Piero Dorazio, Achille Perilli, Pietro Consagra, Giuseppe Capogrossi, Antonio Corpora, Leoncillo Leonardi and so on. Naturally, as was the case within architecture, significant contributions were also made by many lesser-known artists with great artisanal skill (such as Salvatore Meli, Nino Caruso, Michelangelo Conte and Alterige Giorgi). In the *palazzine*, the new abstract vocabulary translated into geometric designs that would form subtly coloured iron textures for street gates or balcony balustrades. However, the preferred space for artistic experimentation was the entrance hall, given its function as filter and passageway between the external public space and the internal private sphere, and as the space designated to confer prestige on all those who inhabit it. For the most part, these interventions were colourful mosaic panels depicting abstract designs or, more rarely, figurative bas-reliefs in marble. Sometimes they extended to specific functional but visibly imposing architectural features (such as columns),[9] or banisters in unusual shapes, perhaps geometric or helicoidal, or details such as frames, handles, flower boxes or wall lights. Not mass produced, these were all one-off pieces for site-specific interventions and unique *palazzine*, each different to the last both externally and internally. The discreet and refined decoration speaks of technical craftsmanship, the result of ancient local, and sometimes even family tradition (as in the case of the mosaics by Andrea and Pietro Cascella who worked with Anna Maria Sforza Cesarini). The extraordinary inventive freedom of these "auteur" interventions, unexpected presences that softened the space, added a unique and original character to bourgeois accommodation in Rome. The high typological and formal quality of many Roman *palazzine* is due precisely to the establishment of this fruitful conversation between art and architecture, especially in the atriums, which are occasionally new and surprising and always elegant and light. It is a heritage just waiting to be discovered, perhaps even restored, but in any case to be valued as a qualifying element of the urban landscape. The photographs in this book show some of its most significant examples.

1 Malatesta, Stefano, *Quando Roma era un paradiso* (Geneva-Milan: Skira, 2015), 25

2 Arbasino, Alberto, *Ritratti italiani* (Milan: Adelphi, 2014), 118-119

3 De Simone, Rosario, *Il dibattito architettonico in Italia negli anni della ricostruzione* (Palermo: Mazzone, 1979), 14. A central figure in this context was Bruno Zevi, who in 1944 founded the APAO or Association for Organic Architecture (cf. E. Cristallini, "Zevi e il dialogo tra arte e architettura negli anni '50" in *Bruno Zevi e la didattica dell'architettura*, edited by P.O. Rossi. Quodlibet, 2018).

4 Regarding the dialogue between art and architecture, cf. E. Cristallini, *Dialoghi tra arte e architettura negli anni della ricostruzione 1945-1955*, (Rome: Gangemi, 2017).

5 This is one of the themes explored by Luigi Moretti and art critic Michel Tapié in the book *Le Baroque généralisé. Manifeste du Baroque Ensembliste*, Turin, 1965.

6 For example, the work of Moretti, who reabsorbed different declinations of art into his own language. This was the case for the Palazzina del Girasole on Via Bruno Buozzi in the Parioli neighbourhood, crowned by a solemn asymmetric tympanum, sliced through by the exposed main staircase and with a pedestal where slabs with finely engraved geometrical designs alternate with slightly protruding slabs of rough "brut" travertine. Later, he would collaborate with American artist Claire Falkenstein and her organic gates and sculptures (the office buildings on Via Morgagni and Piazzale Flaminio in Rome, Villa La Saracena in Santa Marinella).

7 Cf. D. Fonti, "Le arti decorative nel decennio della 'ricostruzione'", in *Roma 1948-1959. Arte, cronaca e cultura dal neorealismo alla dolce vita*, edited by M. Fagiolo dell'Arco and C. Terenzi (Geneva-Milan: Skira, 2002).

8 Severini, already an important figure in the rebirth of sacred art thanks to the creation of decorative murals in various Swiss churches, was asked to collaborate with the Monaco e Luccichenti architect studio on various occasions, creating large panels of elegant and dynamic graphics and bright colours (the Palazzo dei Congressi entrance hall in the EUR district, the Giampaoli sports shop on Via del Corso, headquarters of KLM on Via Barberini).

9 This was the case of Dorazio and Perilli who applied a wall "light" to a pillar in a *palazzina* by Galdieri, establishing a happy dialogue with the environment by way of a subtle play of natural and artificial light. It is a weave of soft concave oblong shapes in grey-white *marmoridea* (a sort of "poor" artificial marble, made of plaster and stone powder, with pearlescent reflections), in contrast with other overhanging shapes in blue painted metal sheet, which look as though they are suspended thanks to the neon underlighting.

8/ 9 Quartiere Montesacro Alto, Bufalotta – Via Roberto Musil – Paolo Portoghesi, 2008

10 Quartiere Gianicolense – Via Isacco Newton – Pier Giorgio Stefani (with Maria Salvaggio and Fiora Lulli), 1972

11 Rione Celio – Via Capo d'Africa, 1950s

12/ 13 Quartiere Prenestino Labicano – Piazzale Prenestino, 1950s/60s

14 (top) Zona Torre Maura – Via Bruno Rizzieri, 1970s

14 (bottom) Quartiere Portuense – Via di Vigna Due Torri – Pier Giorgio Stefani (with Maria Salvaggio and Fiora Lulli), 1973

16 Quartiere Appio Latino – Via Gallia, 1950s

17 Quartiere Trieste – Via della Giuba, mid 1950s

19 Quartiere Ostiense – Piazza Giancarlo Vallauri

21 (top) Quartiere Nomentano – Via Luigi Pulci

21 (bottom) Suburbio Della Vittoria – Via Mario Fani

22/ 23 Quartiere Gianicolense – Via del Vascello, 1950s/60s

25 Quartiere Tuscolano – Via di Acqua Donzella, 1957

26 Quartiere Trionfale, Balduina – Via Ugo de Carolis – Alessandro Tagliolini, 1965

27 Quartiere Aurelio – Via S. Bernadette, 1950s

28/ 29 Quartiere Aurelio – Via Anastasio II

30/ 31 Zona Cassia, Tomba di Nerone – Via San Godenzo – Alessandro Tagliolini, late 1960s/early 1970s

32 Quartiere Parioli – Via Bruxelles – Venturino Ventura, 1968

33 Quartiere Portuense – Largo Gaetano della Loggia – Pier Giorgio Stefani (with Maria Salvaggio and Fiora Lulli), 1970

34 Quartiere Nomentano – Via Luigi Ungarelli – Serena Boselli (ceramic wall panel *Il gioco dell'oca*), 1959-62

35 Quartiere Appio Latino – Via Concordia – Bruno De Caroli most likely in collaboration with Edgardo Mannucci, 1950

36/ 37 Mostacciano – Via Fulvio Tomassucci – Serena Boselli, 1972-75

38 Quartiere Portuense – Largo Gaetano della Loggia – Pier Giorgio Stefani (with Maria Salvaggio and Fiora Lulli), 1970

39 Quartiere Ostiense – Largo Luigi Antonelli, first half of 1960s

40/ 41 Quartiere Nuovo Salario, Val Melaina – Via Giacomo Coppola di Musitani – Serena Boselli, 1968-74

42 Quartiere Trieste Africano – Via Fezzan, early 1950s

43 Quartiere Trieste Africano – Via Senafè, 1974

44/ 45 Quartiere Portuense – Via di Vigna Due Torri – Pier Giorgio Stefani (with Maria Salvaggio and Fiora Lulli), 1973

47 Quartiere Ardeatino – Via Leon Pancaldo

48/ 49 Quartiere Trieste – Via Alfonso Rendano – Serena Boselli, 1953-54

50/ 51 Quartiere Portuense – Via di Vigna Due Torri – Pier Giorgio Stefani (with Maria Salvaggio and Fiora Lulli), 1973

52 Mostacciano – Via Fulvio Tomassucci – Serena Boselli, 1972-75

53 Quartiere Tor di Quinto, Vigna Stelluti – Via Stefano Jacini, early 1960s

54/ 55 Quartiere Trionfale, Balduina – Via Mario Romagnoli – Palazzina designed by Cesare Pascoletti, 1953

56/ 57 Quartiere Pinciano – Via dei Monti Parioli – Marble bas-relief *Orpheus charming the animals with his music* by Alterige Giorgi, 1950s

58 Quartiere della Vittoria – Via Ciro Menotti – Venturini Ventura, 1959

59 Quartiere Appio Latino – Via Apulia

60/ 61 Suburbio Della Vittorie – Via Mario Fani

63 Quartiere Montesacro – Via Vallarsa, 1950s

64/ 65 Quartiere Nomentano – Via Rodolfo Lanciani – Serena Boselli, 1958-61

67 Quartiere Tuscolano – Via Terni – Ceramic panel by Salvatore Meli, 1950s

68 Rione Esquilino – Via Santa Croce in Gerusalemme, early 1970s

69 Quartiere Portuense – Via di Vigna Due Torri – Pier Giorgio Stefani (with Maria Salvaggio and Fiora Lulli), 1973

70/ 71 Quartiere Parioli – Via Fratelli Ruspoli – Ugo Luccichenti, 1949

73 Quartiere Gianicolense – Via Ippolito Nievo – Julio Lafuente, 1973-77

74/ 75 Quartiere Aurelio – Via dei Monti di Creta – Banister most likely designed by Serena Boselli, 1950s

76 Quartiere Aurelio – Via di Boccea, 10, 1960s

77 Quartiere Pinciano – Alberto Carpiceci, 1948

79 Quartiere Appio Latino – Via Concordia – Bruno De Caroli most likely in collaboration with Edgardo Mannucci, 1950

80 Quartiere Montesacro Alto, Talenti – Via Arturo Graf – Giuseppe Castelnuovo, 1970

81 Quartiere Della Vittoria – Via Ciro Menotti Mario Stara (with Giancarlo Pennestri), 1976-78

83 Quartiere Nomentano – Via Luigi Ungarelli – Serena Boselli (ceramic wall panel *Il gioco dell'oca*), 1959-62

84 Rione Celio – Via Capo d'Africa, 1950s

87 Quartiere Europa – EUR Viale – Beethoven Palazzina by Giorgio Calza Bini, stucco wall panelling by Luigi Scirocchi, 1956

88 Quartiere Nomentano – Via Lorenzo il Magnifico – Ceramic artwork signed by Ceramiche Artistiche "Scilla" Via Sirte 31/33 Roma G. Pietracatella, 1955/56

89 Quartiere Nomentano – Via Lorenzo il Magnifico – Ceramic artwork signed by Ceramiche Artistiche "Scilla" Via Sirte 31/33 Roma G. Pietracatella, 1955/56

91 Quartiere Aurelio – Via dei Gozzadini – Vassili Silvio Biuzzi, 1954

92/ 93 Quartiere Trionfale, Balduina – Via Placido Martini, late 1950s/early 1960s

Architects and artists

Biuzzi, Vassili Silvio · Colle Val d'Elsa 1921 – Roma 1987 · Architect
Boselli, Serena · Roma 1922 – Roma 2018 · Architect and artist
Carpiceci, Alberto · Roma 1916 – Roma 2007 · Architect
Castelnuovo, Giuseppe · Roma 1935 – Roma 2020 · Architect
De Caroli, Bruno · Roma 1915 – Roma 1995 · Architect
Lafuente, Julio · Madrid 1921 – Roma 2013 · Architect
Giorgi, Alterige · Codena 1885 – Carrara 1970 · Sculptor
Lucchichenti, Ugo · Isola Liri 1899 – Roma 1976 · Engineer
Mannucci, Edgardo · Roma 1904 – Arcevia 1986 · Sculptor
Meli, Salvatore · Comiso 1929 – Roma 2011 · Sculptor
Pascoletti, Cesare · Povoletto 1898 – Roma 1986 · Architect
Scirocchi, Luigi · Roma 1905 – Roma 1989 · Sculptor
Stefani, Piergiorgio · Val d'Astico 1939 · Architect
Tagliolini, Alessandro · Roma 1931 – Pietrasanta 2000 · Sculptor and painter
Ventura, Venturini · Firenze 1910 – Roma 1991 · Architect

Biographies

Heiner Thofern, born in 1959 in Bielefeld, Germany, was the Deputy Permanent Representative of the Federal Republic of Germany to the United Nations Organizations in Rome from 2015 until 2021. Previously he worked with the Food and Agriculture Organization of the United Nations (FAO) in Rome and with the German Federal Ministry of Food and Agriculture in Bonn and Berlin. Already as a doctoral law student, Thofern cultivated a passion for architecture and town planning. His interests lie in the architecture following the Second World War, particularly that of Italy.

Elisabetta Cristallini is an art critic and historian; she teaches contemporary art history as associate professor at the University of Tuscia in Viterbo and Sapienza University of Rome. She is the author of essays and monographs on the relationship between art and architecture from the 1920s to the 1960s, on international artists of the twentieth century, on post-war art to the most recent artistic experiences, and on environmental and public art. She has curated exhibitions in Italy and in Europe, as well as the scientific project of the Holy See Pavilion at the 56th Venice Biennale in 2015. Her publications include: *Paesaggi incompiuti. Verso un nuovo glossario*; *Dialoghi tra arte e architettura negli anni della ricostruzione 1945-1955*; *L'arte fuori dal museo. Saggi e interviste*; *Kepoi. Giardini d'artista nella Tuscia*; *Nata dall'arte. Gibellina una città per una società estetica.*

Editorial

This book explores a uniquely Roman type of building, the *palazzina* — a four- or five-storey residential structure of the most meticulous design, built during the Italian economic miracle between the 1950s and 1970s. *Beautiful Games* focuses on the extraordinarily imaginative entrances of these buildings.

Over many years, Heiner Thofern photographed *palazzine* during his evening wanderings throughout the north and west districts of Rome. It was their intricately conceived and constructed entrances, realised mostly through collaborations between architects and artists, that particularly caught his eye. *Beautiful Games* reveals the varied treasures of Thofern's photographic archive, a rich collection that allows us to examine the particular sense of play and passion for beauty that shapes this era of Italian creativity, a delight in *la bella figura*, and a desire to constantly reinvent the possibilities of design and architecture.

Ute Eskildsen

Acknowledgements

This book could not have been published without the support from a variety of people. I am profoundly grateful to Gerhard Steidl for his courageous decision to turn a number of my photographs into a book. My special thanks go to the former director of the German Academy in Rome Villa Massimo, Joachim Blüher, who put me in contact with Ute Eskildsen and Timm Rautert. They generously encouraged me to embark on this endeavour and very diligently accompanied the project. My great appreciation is extended to Elisabetta Cristallini for spontaneously agreeing to contribute an enlightening essay to this volume. I also wish to express my gratitude to the architects Massimo and Alberto Parboni Arquati for a very insightful encounter in June 2019. Likewise, I owe my thanks to the architect Pier Giorgio Stefani for a truly inspiring conversation in December 2020. Furthermore, I am very appreciative of Daniele Castelnuovo, Angelo Ferrante, Vincenzo Giorgi and Luca Misici Falzi who provided me with useful information on a number of architects and buildings. Last but not least, my thanks go to my wife Anna and my sons Federico and Lorenzo who have shown remarkable patience that allowed me to explore Rome off the beaten track.

First edition published in 2023

Book design: Ute Eskildsen and Paloma Tarrío Alves / Steidl Design
Separations by Steidl image department
Production and printing: Steidl, Göttingen

Steidl
Düstere Str. 4 / 37073 Göttingen, Germany
Phone +49 551 49 60 60
mail@steidl.de
steidl.de

ISBN 978-3-96999-060-5
Printed in Germany by Steidl